SCOTTISH SONGS AND BALLADS

Nancy Marshall

Chambers

Published 1990 by W & R Chambers Ltd,
43-45 Annandale Street, Edinburgh, EH7 4AZ

British Library Cataloguing in Publication Data

Scottish Songs and ballads.
  1. Ballads in English. Scottish ballads. Words.
  Anthologies
  I. Marshall, Nancy
  821'.044'08

ISBN 0-550-20061-4

Illustrations by John Marshall
Cover design by John Marshall

Typeset by Bookworm Typesetting Ltd, Edinburgh
Printed in Singapore by
Singapore National Printers Ltd

Contents

Preface   v

LOVE

A Red, Red Rose   3
Annie Laurie   4
Afton Water   6
Johnie Faa   8
John Anderson My Jo   11
The Laird o' Cockpen   12
Down the Burn, Davie   14
Jockie Fou and Jenny Fain   15
The Rigs o' Barley   17
Jock of Hazeldean   19
Waly, Waly   20
The Marchioness of Douglas   23
The Banks o' Doon   25
Lassie Lie Near Me   26

LOYALTIES

Lord Maxwell's Goodnight   31
Bruce's Address at Bannockburn   34
Wha'll be King but Charlie?   36
The Land o' the Leal   38
The Campbells are Comin'   40
The Bonnie Earl of Murray   42
Skye Boat Song   44
The Souters of Selkirk   46
Charlie is my Darling   48
The Border Widow's Lament   50
The Queen's Marie   52
The Bonnie House o' Airlie   55
The Flowers of the Forest   57
The Hundred Pipers   59
Will Ye No Come Back Again?   60

CELEBRATION

Rattlin', Roarin' Willie	65
O The Ewe-Bughting's Bonnie	66
The Dusty Miller	68
Green Grow the Rashes	69
O'er the Moor Amang the Heather	71
The Cald Kail of Aberdeen	73
When the Kye Comes Hame	75
My Ain Fireside	77
MacPherson's Farewell	79
Comin' Thro' the Rye	81
For A' That and A' That	83
Kirkdamdie Fair	86
Auld Lang Syne	88
Bibliography	90

Preface

Robert Burns spoke with honesty and simplicity when he said, 'I am delighted with many little melodies which the learned musician despises as silly and stupid.' There are many little melodies between these covers and many beautiful and haunting ones. The sheer volume of old Scottish songs is immense and the great majority are no longer sung by the public at large, as they were in the past. True, we all know the lyrics of Burns' more famous love songs, the loyal Jacobite rally call, and the world over 'Auld Lang Syne' is ritually performed at the end of gatherings, but other equally important works have slipped from everyday usage. The choice for inclusion was difficult. It has been impossible to reproduce some of the longer pieces and lack of space was the only criterion for excluding the music for all.

Looking back on the history of song, it comes through as a vital part of life, the sentiment, whether sad, heroic or downright bawdy, was shared and celebrated by the entire community. Made to be sung, the tunes had to be memorable as they were handed down from one generation to the next. The lyrics varied from one district to another, local features and characters being substituted, but the theme remained essentially the same. Printing had the effect of making the ballads static entities, there being no need to hand down to a subsequent generation something already recorded, and in this way a very special method of communication, both literal and emotional, was lost. James Hogg's mother upbraided Sir Walter Scott for his recording of her songs:

> There war never ane o' my sangs prentit till ye prentit them yoursel', an' ye hae spoilt them awthegither. They were made for singing an' no for reading; but ye hae broken the charm now, an' they'll never be sung mair.

But the taking down and recording of songs by Scott, Burns and others, whilst perhaps robbing them of their 'charm' ensured their survival and place in history. Collectors did alter and substitute verses, but their role was little different from that of previous generations, since they passed on in individual written form what their ancestors had done orally and collectively.

The book is divided into three sections: Love, Loyalties and Celebration. Some of the love lyrics are tender, others by comparison amusing, while the celebratory songs range from the raucous to the profound. The Loyalties section was the most difficult to compile., Murder, treachery and revenge appear alongside many of the wistful tributes to Prince Charles Edward Stuart. Charles' father, James Francis Edward Stuart, was the son of James VII of Scotland and II of England by his second wife Mary of Modena. Many Scots, although by no means all, believed that the Stuarts were the rightful kings and that the Hanoverian line which occupied the throne were the usurpers. Two uprisings, the '15 and the '45, brought them no nearer to their Jacobite inheritance.

This book celebrates all the varied aspects of life felt by generations of the Scottish people for the reader to dip into and enjoy.

LOVE

A RED, RED ROSE

O my luve's like a red, red rose
That's newly sprung in June;
O my luve's like the melodie
That's sweetly play'd in tune.

As fair art thou, my bonnie lass,
So deep in luve am I;
And I will luve thee still, my dear,
Till a' the seas gang dry.

Till a' the seas gang dry, my dear,
And the rocks melt wi' the sun:
O I will love thee still, my dear,
While the sands o' life shall run.

And fare-thee-weel, my only luve!
And fare-thee-weel awhile!
And I will come again, my luve,
Tho' 'twere ten thousand mile!

O my luve's like a red, red rose
That's newly sprung in June;
O my luve's like the melodie
That's sweetly play'd in tune.

This well known and very beautiful old song was originally written by a Lieutenant Hinches as a farewell to his sweetheart. We have no other information about the composer, but we do know that Burns reshaped and improved the original. Burns was also influenced by a song he found in an old anthology written in 1770, with the rather long-winded title 'The Loyal Lover's Farewell to his Sweetheart on Going on a Long Journey'.

ANNIE LAURIE

1st version

Maxwelton banks are bonnie,
Where early fa's the dew,
Where me and Annie Laurie
Made up the promise true;
Made up the promise true,
And ne'er forget will I,
And for bonnie Annie Laurie,
I'd lay down my head and die.

She's backit like a peacock,
She's breastit like a swan,
She's jimp about the middle,
Her waist ye weel may span;
Her waist ye weel may span,
And she has a rolling eye,
And for bonnie Annie Laurie
I'd lay down my head and die.

jimp – slender; *rolling* – spirited

2nd version

Maxwelton braes are bonnie,
Where early fa's the dew,
And it's there that Annie Laurie
Gi'ed me her promise true;
Gi'ed me her promise true,
Which ne'er forgot will be,
And for bonnie Annie Laurie
I'd lay doun my head and dee.

Her brow is like the snaw-drift,
Her throat is like the swan,
Her face it is the bonniest
That e'er the sun shone on.
That e'er the sun shone on,
And dark blue is her e'e.
And for bonnie Annie Laurie
I'd lay doun my head and dee.

Like dew on the gowan lying
Is the fa' o' her fairy feet,
And like winds in summer sighing
Her voice is low and sweet.
Her voice is low and sweet,
And she's a' the world to me;
And for bonnie Annie Laurie
I'd lay doun my head and dee.

gowan – daisy

Annie Laurie was the daughter of Sir Robert Laurie, first
baronet of the Maxwelton family. These lines were
written in praise of her great beauty by William Douglas
of Fingland, Kirkcudbrightshire, some time before 1688.
It would seem that his devotion was not returned as
Annie later married Mr Ferguson of Craigdarroch.

In 1835 an altered and elongated version of this song
was composed by Lady John Scott, a daughter-in-law of
the fourth Duke of Buccleuch. It is shown after the
original and while it is more polished, it lacks the
intensity and essential joy of the first. Lady John would
seem to have created a distant lament, whereas William
Douglas was experiencing the first-hand excitement of
love.

AFTON WATER

Flow gently, sweet Afton, among thy green braes,
Flow gently, I'll sing thee a song in thy praise;
My Mary's asleep by thy murmuring stream
Flow gently, sweet Afton, disturb not her dream.

Thou stock-dove, whose echo resounds thro'
    the glen,
Ye wild whistling blackbirds in yon thorny den,
Thou green-crested lapwing thy screaming forbear,
I charge you disturb not my slumbering fair.

How lofty, sweet Afton, thy neighbouring hills,
Far mark'd with the courses of clear, winding rills;
There daily I wander as noon rises high,
My flocks and my Mary's sweet cot in my eye.

How pleasant thy banks and green valleys below,
Where wild in the woodlands the primroses blow;
There oft as mild ev'ning weeps over the lea,
The sweet scented birk shades my Mary and me.

Thy crystal stream, Afton, how lovely it glides,
And winds by the cot where my Mary resides;
How wanton thy waters her snowy feet lave,
As gathering sweet flowerets she stems thy clear
    wave.

Flow gently, sweet Afton, among thy green braes,
Flow gently, sweet river, the theme of my lays;
My Mary's asleep by thy murmuring stream,
Flow gently, sweet Afton, disturb not her dream!

birk – birch tree

'Afton Water' is one of Burns' best known and best loved
airs. It reflects a pastoral world of simplicity and
tenderness, qualities which Mary Campbell the heroine
herself embodied. Mary or 'Highland Mary' as she
is better known, came into Burns' life when he was
at a low ebb. This slight girl breathed new life and

confidence into the poet. Born in 1768 near Dunoon, where her father was a seaman on board a revenue cutter, she first met Burns when working at Montgomerie Castle as a dairymaid. She caught his eye in Tarbolton Church and a meeting was arranged through a friend. The name 'Highland Mary' originated in this church, where her Gaelic pronunciation of the English Bible was noticeable. The thorn tree at Montgomerie Castle was their regular meeting place and it is known as 'Burns' Thorn' and 'Mary's Tryst'.

In 1786 Burns had thoughts of emigrating to Jamaica and as Mary was returning to her parents' home in Campbeltown, they plighted their troth in the ancient Scottish fashion. Standing facing one another across a tiny stream, they washed their hands as a symbol of purity, before clasping them across the water, holding Mary's Bible between them. This old custom holds that as long as the stream continues to run and as long as the book holds true, then they would be true to one another. They exchanged bibles before saying goodbye for the last time. Mary died of fever in October of that year.

Burns' Bible given to Mary is now in the monument in Alloway, but Mary's to Burns is lost. Their letters are also lost, burned by her brother, when Burns' reputation was in decline and a subsequent embarrassment to the family. The two laments Burns wrote years after her death 'To Mary in Heaven' and 'Highland Mary' are powerful and poignant. He said of her, 'My Highland lassie Mary was a warm hearted, charming young creature as ever blessed a man with generous love.'

JOHNIE FAA

The gypsies cam' to our gude lord's yett,
And O but they sang sweetly;
They sang sae sweet and sae very complete,
That doun cam' our fair lady.

And she cam' tripping down the stair,
And all her maids before her;
As sune as they saw her weel-fa'ured face,
They cuist the glaumourye o'er her.

'O come with me,' says Johnie Faa;
'O come with me, my dearie;
For I vow and I swear by the hilt of my sword,
That your lord shall nae mair come near ye!'

Then she gied them the gude wheit breid,
And they ga'e her the ginger;
But she gied them a far better thing,
The gowd ring aff her finger.

'Gae tak' frae me this gay mantil,
And bring to me a plaidie;
For if kith and kin and a' had sworn,
I'll follow the gipsy laddie.'

'Yestreen I lay in a weel-made bed,
Wi' my gude lord beside me;
This night I'll lie in a tenant's barn,
Whatever shall betide me.'

'Come to your bed,' says Johnie Faa;
'O come to your bed, my dearie;
For I vow and I swear by the hilt of my sword,
That your lord shall nae mair come near ye!'

'I'll go to bed to my Johnie Faa;
I'll go to bed to my dearie;
For I vow and I swear by the fan in my hand,
That my lord shall nae mair come near me.'

'I'll mak' a hap to my Johnie Faa;
I'll mak' a hap to my dearie;
And he's get a' the sash gaes round,
And my lord shall nae mair come near me.'

And when our lord cam' hame at e'en,
And speired for his fair lady,
The tane she cried, and the tither replied,
'She's awa' with the gipsy laddie.'

'Gae saddle to me the black black steed,
Gae saddle and mak' him ready;
Before that I either eat or sleep,
I'll gae seek my fair lady.'

And we were fifteen weel-made men,
Although we were na bonnie;
And we were a' put down for ane,
A fair young wanton lady.

yett – gate; *plaidie* – blanket or shawl; *weel-fa'ured* – good
looking; *cuist* – cast; *glaumourye* – a spell, witchcraft; *hap* –
covering, shelter; *speired* – asked.

There is a great deal of mystery surrounding the origins of
this ballad. Robert Chambers in his *Picture of Scotland*
assigns the role of the lady to Lady Jean Hamilton, wife of
John, the sixth Earl of Cassilis. Whilst one version of the
story, like the ballad, infers that she ran off with a gypsy,
Chambers maintains that the man involved was Sir John
Faa of Dunbar, a former suitor disguised as a gypsy.
    With a band of accomplices Sir John seized the lady
from Cassilis Castle, near Maybole, but was soon
captured at the ford on the River Doon by the returning
Earl and his men. Lady Jean was made to watch from a
window of the castle as her lover and his followers were
hanged from 'The Dule Tree', the gallows of Cassilis
Castle. Thereafter she was imprisoned in Maybole
Castle, where carved heads of the hanged men adorned
a newly added staircase. Here she is said to have
produced enough tapestry to cover all the walls, though

not one stitch remains to prove this. The Countess died in 1642 and letters of the time by her husband to his friends describe her with warmest affection as his 'deir bedfellow' seemingly denying her flight and subsequent imprisonment. But tradition has it that two portraits of the Countess hung at Cassilis, one before her marriage and one after her imprisonment, showing her in tears.

We cannot doubt that the ballad is founded on fact, but the principal actors raise some curious questions. Johnie Faa was no imaginary character. He existed and was universally known as King of the Gypsies or the 'Erle of Little Egypt'. In 1540 he was granted a Privy Seal by King James V giving him authority over his tribe. Those who would associate him with the Cassilis legend could be confusing him with Captain Johnie Faa hanged in 1624 in Edinburgh. If he was one and the same he would have been well over 100 by the time of the deed. This would also suggest that the Countess, born in 1607, had by the age of seventeen produced three children.

We can only imagine that if Johnie Faa, the King of the Gypsies was involved, the events happened at a much earlier date and that the lady, although maybe a Cassilis, was not Lady Jean, or, as Chambers suggests, that at a later date Sir John Faa disguised as a gypsy did come to rescue his former love. Were the Earl's letters created to hide a family secret and do the song and the weeping portrait tell the true tale?

JOHN ANDERSON MY JO

John Anderson my jo, John,
When we were first acquent;
Your locks were like the raven,
Your bonie brow was brent;
But now your brow is beld, John
Your locks are like the snaw;
But blessings on your frosty pow,
John Anderson my jo!

John Anderson my jo, John,
We clamb the hill thegither;
And mony a canty day John,
We've had wi' ane anither;
Now we maun totter down, John,
And hand in hand we'll go;
And sleep thegither at the foot,
John Anderson my jo!

brent – smooth and high; *beld* – bald; *pow* – head; *canty* –
cheerful, happy

Verses from the original have been discovered in a
manuscript dated 1560, belonging to Bishop Percy, but
compared to this version by Burns they appear crude
and coarse. Later attempts to add extra verses have also
failed to equal Burns. John Anderson was the town piper
of Kelso and a well known Borders character.

THE LAIRD O' COCKPEN

Air – 'When she cam' ben, she bobbit'.

The Laird o' Cockpen, he's proud an' he's great,
His mind is ta'en up wi' things o' the State;
He wanted a wife, his braw house to keep,
But favour wi' wooin' was fashious to seek.

Down by the dyke-side a lady did dwell,
At his table-head he thought she'd look well,
McClish's ae daughter o' Clavers-ha' Lee,
A penniless lass wi' a lang pedigree.

His wig was weel pouther'd and as gude as new,
His waistcoat was white, his coat it was blue;
He put on a ring, a sword, and cock'd hat,
And wha could refuse the Laird wi' a' that?

He took the grey mare, and rade cannily,
An' rapp'd at the yett o' Clavers-ha' Lee;
'Gae tell Mistress Jean to come speedily ben, –
She's wanted to speak to the Laird o' Cockpen.'

Mistress Jean was makin' the elder-flower wine;
'An what brings the Laird at sic a like time?'
She put aff her apron, and on her silk gown,
Her mutch wi' red ribbons, and gaed awa' down.

An' when she cam' ben he bowed fu' low,
An' what was his errand he soon let her know;
Amazed was the Laird when the lady said 'Na,'
And wi' a laigh curtsie she turned awa'.

Dumfounder'd was he, nae sigh did he gie,
He mounted his mare – he rade cannily;
An' aften he thought, as he gaed through the glen,
She's daft to refuse the Laird o' Cockpen.

And now that the Laird his exit had made,
Mistress Jean she reflected on what she had said;
'Oh, for ane I'll get better, its waur I'll get ten,
I was daft to refuse the Laird o' Cockpen.'

Next time that the Laird and the lady were seen,
They were gaun arm-in-arm to the kirk on the green;
Now she sits in the ha' like a weel-tappit hen,
But as yet there's nae chickens appear'd at Cockpen.

fashious – troublesome; *mutch* – a cap; *pouther'd* –
powdered; *laigh* – low; *weel-tappit hen* – proud and well
contented lady.

The older version of this song was simply called
'Cockpen' and belongs to the reign of Charles II. This
version by Lady Nairne was composed at the House of
Gask in her youth. The first seven stanzas are hers, the
last two being the work of Susan Ferrier.

The Laird of Cockpen lived at the Court of King
Charles, when it was in exile at the Hague. He was a fine
musician, producing many songs for the King's
amusement. In particular, 'Brose and Butter', with
which he was commanded to lull the King to sleep at
night and awaken him in the morning. After the
Restoration Cockpen discovered his estate had been
confiscated, because of his allegiance to the King.
Repeated requests for its reinstatement were denied.
Refused a meeting with the King, he devised a ploy to cut
through the network of courtiers.

The organist at the Chapel Royal was persuaded to
allow the Laird to deputise for him at the next service.
Towards the end, as the congregation was filing out,
Cockpen leapt into a vigorous rendition of 'Brose and
Butter'. His plan succeeded, the King immediately
appearing in the organ gallery declaring that the music
'almost made him dance'.

Cockpen's request was fulfilled and his lands were
restored.

DOWN THE BURN, DAVIE

When trees did bud, and fields were green,
And broom bloom'd fair to see;
When Mary was complete fifteen,
And love laugh'd in her eye;
Blyth Davie's blinks her heart did move
To speak her mind thus free,
Gang down the burn, Davie, love,
And I will follow thee.

Now Davie did each lad surpass,
That dwelt on this burn-side,
And Mary was the bonniest lass,
Just meet to be a bride:
Her cheeks were rosy, red, and white,
Her een were bonny blue;
Her looks were like Aurora bright,
Her lips like dropping dew.

As down the burn they took their way,
What tender tales they said!
His cheek to hers he aft did lay,
And with her bosom play'd;
Till baith at length impatient grown
To be mair fully blest,
In yonder vale they lean'd them down; –
Love only saw the rest.

What pass'd, I guess, was harmless play,
And naething sure unmeet;
For, ganging hame, I heard them say,
They lik'd a walk sae sweet;
And that they aften shou'd return
Sic pleasure to renew.
Quoth Mary, love, I like the burn,
And ay shall follow you.

In the past this old song, written by Robert Crawford, has been considered somewhat blunt, particularly the last two verses. On request, and probably not of choice, Burns attempted an alteration, removing the 'offending' lines by leaving out the last half of the third stanza and the first half of the fourth. Despite this censoring it has happily survived intact, its sentiments untainted by puritanical prudery. The tune is old and the original words were probably very different. Burns ascribed the composition to David Maigh, Keeper of Blood Hounds to Riddell of Tweeddale. The song is as ancient as the post held by Maigh.

JOCKIE FOU AND JENNY FAIN

Jockie fou and Jenny fain,
Jenny was nae ill to gain;
She was couthy, he was kind, —
Thus the wooer tell'd his mind,
Jenny, I'll nae mair be nice —
Gie me love at ony price;
I'll ne'er stand for red or white,
Love alane can give delight.

Ithers seek, they kenna what,
Features, carriage, and a' that;
Gie me love in her I court,
Love to love makes a' the sport;
Let love sparkle in her ee,
Let her love nae man but me, —
That's the tocher gude I prize,
There the lover's treasure lies.

Colours mingled unco fine,
Common motives lang sinsyne,
Never can engage my love –
Let my fancy first approve:
'Tis na' meat but appetite
Makes our eating a delight –
Beauty is at best deceit,
Fancy only kens nae cheat.

fou – drunk; *fain* – eager; *couthy* – tender; *tocher* – dowry;
gude – large, considerable; *lang sinsyne* – long ago

The author of this witty song is unknown, but it would appear to be very old. Jockie's amusing directness and honesty, although released by the effects of alcohol, contain more than a few gems on the wisdom of following one's instincts. He and 'eager' Jenny have a deeper bond than the genteel lovers of better known songs.

THE RIGS O' BARLEY

It was upon a Lammas night,
When corn rigs are bonie,
Beneath the moon's unclouded light,
I held awa to Annie:
The time flew by, wi' tentless heed,
Till 'tween the late and early;
Wi' sma' persuasion she agreed,
To see me thro' the barley.

    Corn rigs, an' barley rigs,
    An' corn rigs are bonie:
    I'll ne'er forget that happy night,
    Amang the rigs wi' Annie.

The sky was blue, the wind was still,
The moon was shining clearly;
I set her down, wi' right good will,
Amang the rigs o' barley:
I ken't her heart was a' my ain;
I lov'd her most sincerely;
I kiss'd her owre and owre again,
Amang the rigs o' barley.

    Corn rigs, an' barley etc.

I lock'd her in my fond embrace;
Her heart was beating rarely:
My blessings on that happy place,
Amang the rigs o' barley!
But by the moon and stars so bright,
That shone that night so clearly!
She ay shall bless that happy night,
Amang the rigs o' barley.

    Corn rigs, an' barley etc.

I hae been blythe wi' Comrades dear;
I hae been merry drinking;
I hae been joyfu' gath'rin gear;
I hae been happy thinking;
But a' the pleasures e'er I saw,
Tho' three times doubl'd fairly,
That happy night was worth them a',
    Amang the rigs o' barley.

    Corn rigs, an' barley etc.

Lammas night – 1st August; *tentless* – careless; *gath'rin gear*
– making money

This song dates from Burns' early life at Lochlea Farm.
Poor, by Ayrshire standards, it was nonetheless better
than the previous tenancy at Mount Oliphant, where the
soil barely covered the rocks beneath. This ode to
midsummer and also to Annie reflects a more hopeful
period in his younger life. He considered the last verse to
be the best he had ever written, coming nearest to his
ideal of 'poetical perfection'.
    One of Burns' neighbours at Lochlea was John
Rankine, a farmer at Adamhill. His youngest daughter
Anne is believed to be the heroine, but in later years
most of the Annies of the district claimed the right.

JOCK OF HAZELDEAN

Why weep ye by the tide, ladye —
Why weep ye by the tide?
I'll wed ye to my youngest son,
And ye shall be his bride;
And ye shall be his bride, ladye,
Sae comely to be seen —
But ay she loot the tears down fa'
For Jock of Hazeldean.

Now let this wilful grief be done,
And dry that cheek so pale,
Young Frank is chief of Errington,
And lord of Langley-dale:
His step is first in peaceful ha',
His sword is battle keen —
But ay she loot the tears down fa'
For Jock of Hazeldean.

A chain of gold ye shall not lack,
Nor braid to bind your hair,
Nor mettled hound, nor managed hawk,
Nor palfrey fresh and fair;
And you the foremost of them a'
Shall ride — our forest queen —
But ay she loot the tears down fa'
For Jock of Hazeldean.

The kirk was deck'd at morning tide,
The tapers glimmer'd fair,
The priest and bridegroom wait the bride,
And knight and dame are there:
They sought her both by bower and ha',
The ladye was not seen —
She's o'er the border, and awa'
Wi' Jock of Hazeldean.

The original of this song is a compilation of different ballads in a romantic vein. Hearing only a fragment of it Sir Walter Scott embarked upon his own version and produced a shorter, more amusing song. Using the name of a place in Roxburghshire, he changed the title from the original 'Jock of Hazelgreen' to 'Jock of Hazeldean'.

WALY, WALY

O waly, waly up the bank,
And waly, waly down the brae,
And waly, waly by yon burnside,
Where I and my love were wont to gae!
I leant my back into an aik,
I thought it was a trusty tree;
But first it bow'd and syne it brak',
Sae my true love did lightly me.

O waly, waly, gin love be bonny,
A little time while it is new,
But when it's auld, it waxeth cauld,
And fades away like morning dew.
O wherefore should I busk my head?
Or wherefore should I kaim my hair?
For my true love has me forsook,
And says he'll never lo'e me mair.

Now Arthur's Seat shall be my bed,
The sheets shall ne'er be pressed by me:
Saint Anton's Well shall be my drink,
Since my true love's forsaken me.
Martinmas wind, when wilt thou blaw,
And shake the green leaves aff the tree?
O gentle death, when wilt thou come?
For of my life I am wearie!

'Tis not the frost that freezes fell,
Nor blawing snaw's inclemencie;
'Tis not sic cauld that makes me cry,
But my love's heart grown cauld to me.
When we cam' in by Glasgow toun,
We were a comely sight to see;
My love was clad i' the black velvet,
And I mysell in cramoisie.

But had I wist before I kiss'd,
That love had been sae ill to win,
I had lock'd my heart in a case of gowd,
And pinn'd it wi' a siller pin.
Oh, oh! if my young babe were born,
And set upon the nurse's knee,
And I mysell were dead and gane,
For a maid again I'll never be!

waly, waly – alas, a lamentation; *aik* – oak; *syne* – then;
busk – dress, decorate; *kaim* – comb; *cramoisie* – crimson;
gowd – gold ·

Believed to be one of the oldest and finest Scottish ballads, 'Waly, Waly' was written before 1566. A manuscript of this date has revealed some of the more famous lines of the song. Robert Chambers initially believed it referred to an incident at the court of Mary Queen of Scots, but latterly, on finding references in the Pepysian Library at Cambridge, he attributed it to a later date and to an event in 1670 involving the Marchioness of Douglas. 'Waly, Waly' and 'The Marchioness of Douglas' are in fact two separate ballads. 'The Marchioness of Douglas' contains some of the lines and verses from 'Waly, Waly' but we can assume that the later composer merely adopted these from the existing song, as and when they suited the actions and sentiments of his tale.

The Marchioness of Douglas, formerly Lady Barbara Erskine, was the eldest daughter of John, ninth Earl of Mar. She married James Douglas, second Marquis of Douglas in 1670, but their happiness was cut short, because of the plotting of Lowrie, the tutor or laird of Blackwood, who was chamberlain to the Marquis. A rejected suitor of Lady Barbara, Lowrie had his revenge by falsely accusing the Marchioness of adultery. Even at the eleventh hour a reconciliation was possible, but Lowrie's continued onslaught of lies ensured the separation would be for ever. Rescued by her father, the Marchioness never saw her husband again. The only son of the marriage, James, Earl of Angus, was later killed at the Battle of Steinkirk.

The following verses from the song describe the plot and also show where the lines have been adopted from the earlier work.

THE MARCHIONESS OF DOUGLAS

I was a lady of high renown,
As lived in the north countrie;
I was a lady of high renown,
When Earl Douglas loved me.

When we cam thro' Glasgow toun
We were a comely sight to see;
My gude lord in velvet green,
And I mysel in cramoisie.

When that my auld son was born,
And set upon the nurse's knee,
I was happy woman as e'er was born,
And my gude lord he loved me.

There cam a man into this house,
And Jamie Lockhart was his name;
And it was tauld to my gude lord,
That I was in the bed wi' him.

There cam anither to this house,
And a bad friend he was to me!
He put Jamie's shoon below my bed-stock,
And bade my gude lord come and see.

O wae be unto thee, Blackwood!
And aye an ill death may ye die!
For ye was the first and the foremost man,
That parted my gude lord and me.

'O fare-thee-weel, my once lovely maid;
O fare-thee-weel, once dear to me!
O fare-thee-weel, my once lovely maid,
For wi' me again ye shall never be!'

When my father he heard word,
That my gude lord had forsaken me;
He sent fifty o' his brisk dragoons,
To fetch me hame to my ain countrie.

'O fare-thee-weel, Jamie Douglas!
And fare-ye-weel, my children three;
I hope your father may prove more kind
To you than he has been to me!'

O, an I had my baby born,
And set upon the nurse's knee;
And I mysel were dead and gane,
For a maid again I'll never be!

THE BANKS O' DOON

Ye banks and braes o' bonie Doon,
How can ye bloom sae fresh and fair!
How can ye chant, ye little birds,
And I sae weary, fu' o' care!

Thou'll break my heart, thou warbling bird,
That wantons thro' the flowering thorn;
Thou minds me o' departed joys,
Departed never to return.

Oft hae I rov'd by bonie Doon,
To see the rose and woodbine twine;
And ilka bird sang o' its luve,
And fondly sae did I o' mine.

Wi' lightsome heart I pu'd a rose,
Fu' sweet upon its thorny tree;
And my fause luver staw my rose,
But, ah! he left the thorn wi' me.

Staw – stole

Burns celebrated the youth and beauty of Peggy Kennedy in 'Young Peggy', but it was his lament for her lost innocence in 'The Banks o' Doon' which captured the public's imagination. The tune is beautiful, which is one reason for its popularity, but perhaps also the theme of loss and tragedy has a stronger appeal than the worship of beauty.

Born in Ayrshire in 1768, Peggy was the daughter of Robert Kennedy of Daljarrock and just seventeen when she became engaged to Captain Andrew McDowall of Logan. A 'secret' marriage ceremony was never legalised and after giving birth to a daughter, she was abandoned by McDowall, who subsequently married a Dumfriesshire laird's daughter. In 1795 Peggy brought a court action against McDowall in an attempt to have the marriage recognised, but she died before it was concluded. Three years later the Constitutional Court of the Church declared the marriage legal, but on appeal to the Court of Session, McDowall had this reversed. An award of £3,000 was eventually made to Peggy's daughter in lieu of damages suffered by her mother.

LASSIE LIE NEAR ME

Lang have we parted been,
Lassie, my dearie;
Now we are met again,
Lassie lie near me.
Near me, near me,
Lassie lie near me:
Lang hast thou lain thy lane,
Lassie lie near me.

The dangers of battle, love,
How could they fear me?
Thy wishes were with me,
And fate wadna steer me.
Near me, near me,
Lassie lie near me:
I woo'd thee and wedded thee,
Lassie lie near me.

O, seven lang summers
Thy love had to sue thee;
And, seven years banish'd,
Again maun I woo thee?
Woo thee, woo thee;
Ay, look on thy husband, love,
Say, maun he woo thee?

When, for thy love, lassie,
Lord William he dared me,
Oh! was it not sad, that
His sharp weapon spared me?
Spared me, spared me;
Now for to see thee,
As a lark with the raven,
Thus ready to flee me?

She gave one wild look such
As man never painted;
With a wild sob of joy
In his bosom she fainted.
My love, O my love –
My own blessed Annie! –
Their looks were fu' tender,
Their words were nae many.

lain thy lane – lain alone; *maun* – must

This song has suffered many alterations and additions.
The title was changed from 'Laddie, Lie Near Me' to the
supposedly less suggestive 'Lassie, Lie Near Me' or the
even more delicate 'Wifie, Lie Near Me', while later
versions also take on a Jacobite hue, but the simplicity
and intimacy of the lyrics shine through any attempt at
coyness or political bias to reveal the warm reunion of
two lovers.

The original author is unknown and several pens have
been involved in the subsequent changes, none
fortunately able to tarnish the purity of the initial
sentiment.

LOYALTIES

LORD MAXWELL'S GOODNIGHT

'Adieu, madame, my mother dear,
But and my sisters three!
Adieu, fair Robert of Orchardstane!
My heart is wae for thee.
Adieu, the lily and the rose,
The primrose fair to see:
Adieu, my ladye, and only joy!
For I may not stay with thee.

'Though I hae slain the Lord Johnstone,
What care I for their feid?
My noble mind their wrath disdains:
He was my father's deid.
Both night and day I laboured oft
Of him avenged to be;
But now I've got what lang I sought,
And I may not stay with thee.

'Adieu! Drumlanrig, false wert aye,
And Closeburn in a band!
The Laird of Lag, frae my father that fled,
When the Johnston struck aff his hand.
They were three brethren in a band —
Joy may they never see!
Their treacherous art, and cowardly heart,
Has twin'd my love and me.

'Adieu! Dumfries, my proper place,
But and Carlaverock fair!
Adieu! my castle of the Thrieve,
Wi' a' my buildings there:
Adieu! Lochmaben's gates sae fair,
The Langholm-holm, where birks there be;
Adieu! my ladye, and only joy,
For, trust me, I may not stay wi' thee.

'Adieu! fair Eskdale up and down,
Where my puir friends do dwell;
The bangisters will ding them down,
And will them sair compell.

31

But I'll avenge their feid mysell,
When I come o'er the sea;
Adieu! my ladye, and only joy,
For I may not stay wi' thee.'

'Lord of the land!' — that ladye said,
O wad ye go wi' me,
Unto my brother's stately tower,
Where safest ye may be!
There Hamiltons and Douglas baith,
Shall rise to succour thee.'
'Thanks for thy kindness, fair my dame,
But I may not stay wi' thee.'

Then he tuik aff a gay gold ring,
Thereat hang signets three;
'Hae, take thee that, mine ain dear thing,
And still hae mind o' me;
But, if thou take another lord,
Ere I come ower the sea —
His life is but a three days' lease,
Tho' I may not stay wi' thee.'

The wind was fair, the ship was clear,
That good lord went away;
And most part of his friends were there,
To give him a fair convey.
They drank the wine, they didna spair,
Even in that gude lord's sight —
Sae now he's o'er the floods sae gray,
And Lord Maxwell has ta'en his Goodnight.

wae – sad; *feid* – feud; *deid* – curse, murderer; *false wert aye* – always untrustworthy; *holm* – wood; *birks* – birch trees; *bangisters* – those in power; *ding* – smash

The lyrics of this lovely old ballad convey only a drop of the bitterness and hatred that existed between the two most powerful border families of that time, the Maxwells and the Johnstones. In 1585, John, the sixth Lord Maxwell, was declared a rebel. His old enemy, the Laird of Johnstone, Warden of the West Marches, was commissioned by the King to apprehend him, but the Maxwells routed the Johnstones, setting fire to Lochwood

Castle, the Johnstones' family seat. In a later dispute Johnstone was again defeated and, it is said, died of a broken heart.

The old feud was renewed in 1593 triggered by a cattle-rustling incident, the Johnstones raiding the lands of the Lairds of Crichton, Sanquhar and Drumlanrig, killing anyone in pursuit. This episode is well documented in the ballad 'The Lads of Wamphray'. Needing help to prevent further losses, but hesitant about appealing to Maxwell for assistance, due to his new-found peace with the Johnstones, the Lairds approached him with the suggestion of becoming his liegemen under a bond of manrent, in exchange for his support in their quarrel with the Johnstones. The Maxwells, restored to the King's favour and given the Wardenry of the West Marches, were now ironically commissioned to apprehend the Johnstones.

In the ensuing battle Sir James Johnstone, now chieftain of the clan, supported by the Buccleuchs, Elliots, Armstrongs and Graemes cut a swathe through a party of the Maxwells at Lochmaben. Subsequently Lord Maxwell with 2,000 men invaded Annandale, but for him the battle at Dryffe Sands, near Lockerbie, was a disaster. He was killed and his hand amputated as a trophy of war. Many of his men were lost or injured, especially by slashes across the face, which became known as 'a Lockerbie lick'. To keep the anger burning, the family refused to bury the chieftain's body and it was four years later and then only by royal command that they did so.

John, the seventh Lord Maxwell vowed revenge for his father's death and because of his threats he was barred from the border counties. He attempted to return and was confined to Edinburgh Castle, but he escaped and made his way to Dumfriesshire supposedly with an olive branch for the Johnstones. During his meeting with Sir James on 6 April 1608 a quarrel broke out between their two servants, Maxwell's killing Johnstone's. As Sir James turned to see what was happening, Maxwell shot him twice in the back.

Maxwell escaped to France, but was caught five years later after returning to Caithness. He was beheaded in Edinburgh. The ballad must have been written before this final event as there is no mention of his execution.

BRUCE'S ADDRESS AT BANNOCKBURN

Scots! wha hae wi' Wallace bled,
Scots! wham Bruce has aften led,
Welcome to your gory bed,
Or to victory!
Now's the day and now's the hour;
See the front o' battle lour:
See approach proud Edward's power —
Chains and slavery!

Wha will be a traitor knave?
Wha can fill a coward's grave?
Wha sae base as be a slave?
Let him turn and flee!
Wha for Scotland's king and law
Freedom's sword will strongly draw?
Freeman stand, or freeman fa'?
Let him on wi me!

By oppression's woes and pains!
By your sons in servile chains!
We will drain our dearest veins,
But they shall be free!
Lay the proud usurpers low!
Tyrants fall in every foe!
Liberty's in every blow! —
Let us do or die!
So may God ever defend the cause of truth and
liberty, as he did that day! Amen.

The air 'Hey, tuttie taitie' was believed by many to be
Robert the Bruce's rousing call to arms on the morning of
Bannockburn. Burns was often moved to tears by it and
one evening whilst out walking, he threw his national-
istic fervour into these lyrics, now famous the world
over. He was at one point persuaded to exchange the
old tune for another, but the public preferred his first
choice and continued to sing it in the original form.
  Bannockburn in 1314 was a triumph for the Scots as
their King, Robert the Bruce, led some 8,000 men to
victory over the English army of Edward II totalling at

least 18,000. Burns, visiting the site in 1787, visualised his 'gallant, heroic countrymen, coming o'er the hill and down upon the plunderers of their country.' Almost 500 years after the event his combination of words and music typified the intense patriotism felt by many Scots.

WHA'LL BE KING BUT CHARLIE?

The news frae Moidart cam' yestreen,
Will soon gar mony ferlie;
For ships o' war hae just come in,
And landit Royal Charlie.

Come thro' the heather, around him gather,
Ye're a' the welcomer early;
Around him cling wi' a' your kin;
For wha'll be king but Charlie?
Come thro' the heather, around him gather,
Come Ronald, come Donald, come a' thegither,
And crown your rightfu', lawfu' king!
For wha'll be king but Charlie?

The Hieland clans, wi' sword in hand,
Frae John o' Groats to Airlie,
Hae to a man declared to stand
Or fa' wi' Royal Charlie.

Come thro' the heather etc.

The Lowlands a', baith great an' sma',
Wi' mony a lord and laird, hae
Declar'd for Scotia's king an' law,
An' speir ye what but Charlie.

Come thro' the heather etc.

There's ne'er a lass in a' the lan'
But vows baith late an' early,
She'll ne'er to man gie heart nor han',
Wha wadna fecht for Charlie.

Come thro' the heather etc.

Then here's a health to Charlie's cause,
And be't complete an' early;
His very name our heart's blood warms;
To arms for Royal Charlie!

Come thro' the heather etc.

gar mony ferlie – made many wonder; *speir* – ask

In July 1745 Prince Charles Edward Stuart's ship the *Du Teillay* dropped anchor at Loch nan Uamh, a stretch of water between Moidart and Arisaig. With him from France came the Marquis of Tullibardine, Sir Thomas Sheridan, Sir John Macdonald, Francis Strickland, Mr Kelly (a clergyman), Aeneas Macdonald (a banker in Paris), and Buchanan (the Prince's messenger). In this remote and secluded part of Scotland, Charles was assured of loyalty, but even here many Highland chiefs cautioned against an uprising without guaranteed support within Scotland and external aid from France. Charles, however, knowing there was little chance of help from Louis XV, determined to force through his plans, in the delusion that all Scotsmen would rise to restore their King. By 19 August his standard was unfurled at Glenfinnan and those loyal to him slowly came forward. Barely 15 months later he sailed back to France and safety.

Charles did raise a Highland army, he did take Edinburgh and invade England, but it was because of his blinkered vision of himself combined with a great personal charisma and the immense loyalty of a comparatively small force, rather than the full support of the Scottish nation. The disaster at Culloden was caused chiefly by his stoic refusal to listen to his generals, preferring instead to take advice from his Irish friends. On his insistence a starving, unpaid and understrength Jacobite army took on the might of 9,000 of the government's best troops and were subsequently massacred. His last days in Scotland were spent in hiding, with friends risking imprisonment and death for a man they believed to be their true King. The final image of him is that of a portly, lonely old man languishing in exile.

The authorship of this 'call to arms' for Charlie was unclear for some time, but it is now attributed to Lady Nairne.

THE LAND O' THE LEAL

Air — 'Hey tutti taiti'.

I'm wearin' awa' John,
Like snaw-wreaths in thaw, John,
I'm wearin' awa'
To the land o' the leal.
There's nae sorrow there, John,
There's neither cauld nor care, John,
The day is aye fair
In the land o' the leal.

Our bonnie bairn's there, John,
She was baith gude and fair, John,
And oh! we grudged her sair
To the land o' the leal.
But sorrow's sel' wears past, John,
And joy's a-comin' fast, John,
The joy that's aye to last
In the land o' the leal.

Sae dear's that joy was bought, John,
Sae free the battle fought, John,
That sinfu' man e'er brought
To the land o' the leal.
Oh! dry your glist'ning e'e, John,
My saul langs to be free, John,
And angels beckon me
To the land o' the leal.

Oh! haud ye leal and true, John,
Your day it's wearin' through, John
And I'll welcome you
To the land o' the leal.
Now fare-ye-weel, my ain John,
This warld's cares are vain, John,
We'll meet, and we'll be fain,
In the land o' the leal.

leal — loyal, true; *fain* — fond, affectionate

38

Lady Nairne composed this air in 1798 as a private message of consolation. It commemorates the short life of the much loved baby daughter of Mary Anne Colquhoun, an old friend and distant relative. Mary Anne was the wife of Archibald Campbell Colquhoun, advocate and sheriff of Perthshire. She had previously been admired by the young Walter Scott whilst living with her brother William Erskine in Edinburgh. Scott's hopes were dashed when she decided to marry Colquhoun and by way of explanation she instructed her brother to hand to Scott the day after she was married, a letter, in which she assured him of her fondness, friendship and 'sisterly' feelings. The marriage was a happy one and blessed with a beautiful daughter, who sadly died before her first birthday. She left her parents distraught.

For many years the authorship was a well kept secret. It had been attributed to Burns with 'Jean' substituted for 'John' inferring it was his deathbed address, though never included in his collection. Lady Nairne herself was present at a gathering where this was suggested and said nothing. The pact with an old friend was firmly kept. In later life she maintained that she had merely liked the air and put lyrics to it. But she also described it as 'a happy rest for the mind in this dark pilgrimage'.

Lady Nairne was born Carolina Oliphant. She first came to Edinburgh in 1806, the newly married wife of Major William Murray Nairne, her second cousin. She spent many happy, relaxed days at Ravelston House visiting Alexander Keith and his sister, relatives of Sir Walter Scott and enjoying the company of her old friend Mrs Campbell Colquhoun. Her younger sister Margaret Oliphant married Mr Keith or 'the laddie Sandy' as he was called by his sister until he was in his seventies. Lady Nairne met Sir Walter Scott during her time in Edinburgh, but they remained acquaintances rather than friends.

THE CAMPBELLS ARE COMIN'

The Campbells are comin', O-ho, O-ho!
The Campbells are comin', O-ho, O-ho!
The Campbells are comin' to bonnie Lochleven;
The Campbells are comin', O-ho, O-ho!

Listening to the rousing chorus from 'The Campbells Are Coming', it is not difficult to understand why the air is believed by some to be the Campbells' old marching tune. Its origin is debated, but the lyrics may go back as far as 1567, when Mary Queen of Scots was incarcerated in Lochleven Castle, the Campbells at that time being her loyal supporters.

The song was more probably written around 1715, when John Campbell, Duke of Argyll, led the government forces of George I against the Jacobite army gathering around the Earl of Mar. Two months before the battle of Sheriffmuir, Argyll sought the protection of Stirling Castle with troops totalling a mere 1,500 men. A further 1,000 men from the Campbell militia marched from Argyllshire to join the Duke at Stirling and this would seem the most likely inspiration for the composition. All Argyll's efforts to muster recruits resulted in a force of only 4,000 while the Earl of Mar had 15,000. The Battle of Sheriffmuir was a disaster, due to the incompetence and indecision on both sides, neither being the winner. The rebellion fizzled out after this, the Jacobite army dispersed and by the time the Old Pretender, James Edward Stuart, father of 'Bonnie Prince Charlie', arrived at Perth, the cause was already lost.

THE BONNIE EARL OF MURRAY

Ye Highlands, and ye Lawlands,
Oh, where have ye been?
They hae slain the Earl o' Murray,
And lain him on the green.

'Now wae be to you, Huntly!
And wherefore did ye sae?
I bade you bring him wi' you,
But forbade you him to slay.'

He was a braw gallant,
And he rade at the ring;
And the bonnie Earl o' Murray,
Oh! he micht ha' been a king.

He was a braw gallant,
And he rade at the gluve;
And the bonnie Earl o' Murray,
Oh! he was the Queen's luve!

Oh! lang will his lady
Look ower the Castle Doune,
Ere she see the Earl o' Murray
Come sounding through the toun.

rade – rode

The Earl of Murray, son of Lord Doune, inherited his
title, not through his own family line, but from his wife,
daughter of Regent Moray. Along with the title and the
lands came the legacy of a feud with the Earl of Huntly,
head of the powerful Gordon family. In 1591 Huntly
succeeded in implicating Murray in the Earl of
Bothwell's plot against the crown. James VI, in giving
Huntly the commission to arrest Murray also ensured
the capture of a handsome, accomplished man, much
favoured by his own Queen Anne.

Cornered in his mother's home at Dunnibrissle in
Fife, Murray refused to surrender. The house was
torched and many were killed by Huntly's forces as

they ran from the flames. Murray himself escaped to the shore, but was traced to a cave, where Gordon of Buckie fatally wounded him. To ensure Huntly's complicity in the murder, Gordon demanded he strike the dying earl. As he took a dagger blow in the face Murray assured Huntly, 'You have spoiled a better face than your own.'

Gordon was sent to Edinburgh with the news of Murray's death, while Huntly quietly slipped away to the safety of Ravenscraig Castle, where Lord Sinclair greeted his arrival by exclaiming 'that he was welcome to come in, but would have been twice as welcome to have passed by.' Huntly was later caught, but because of his royal commission could not be held for murder. The Earl of Murray's body lay for many months in the church of Leith, while his friends demanded justice for his death. It was never realised. The writer is unknown and there have been other slightly differing versions, but the song has remained popular.

SKYE BOAT-SONG

Speed, bonnie boat, like a bird on the wing,
Onward the sailors cry;
Carry the lad that's born to be king
Over the sea to Skye.

Loud the winds howl, loud the waves roar,
Thunder-clouds rend the air;
Baffled, our foes stand by the shore,
Follow they will not dare.

   Speed, bonnie boat, &c.

Though the waves leap, soft shall ye sleep;
Ocean's a royal bed.
Rocked in the deep, Flora will keep
Watch by your weary head.

   Speed, bonnie boat, &c.

Many's the lad fought on that day,
Well the claymore could wield,
When the night came silently lay
Dead of Culloden's field.

   Speed, bonnie boat, &c.

Burned are our homes, exile and death
Scatter the loyal men;
Yet ere the sword cool in the sheath,
Charlie will come again.

   Speed, bonnie boat &c.

This salute to Jacobitism embraces the courage and
ingenuity of Flora MacDonald as she escorted 'Bonnie
Prince Charlie' to Skye one stormy night in 1746. With
Charles dressed as Flora's maid, they sailed from
South Uist on 28 June and, as the song says, the seas
were wild and the wind howling. Their first attempt to
land at Waternish in the west corner of Skye proved

impossible with the shore heavily guarded and several men-of-war standing by. Kilbride in Trotternish some twelve miles further north was a safe harbour and from here they went ashore to spend the next twelve days living rough, whilst moving from one 'safe house' to another. When the Prince and Flora said their goodbyes at Portree, General Campbell's men were only a few days behind. Charles escaped once more, but it was some months later before he sailed back to France and safety.

THE SOUTERS OF SELKIRK

Up wi' the Souters o' Selkirk,
And down wi' the fazart Lord Hume!
But up wi' ilka braw callant
That sews the single-soled shoon;
And up wi' the lads o' the Forest
That ne'er to the Southron wad yield;
But deil scoup o' Hume and his menzie,
That stude sae abiegh on the field!

Fye! on the green and the yellow,
The craw-hearted loons o' the Merse;
But here's to the Souters o' Selkirk,
The elshin, the lingle, and birse.
Then up wi' the Souters o' Selkirk,
For they are baith trusty and leal;
And up wi' the lads o' the Forest,
And down wi' the Merse to the deil!

fazart – cowardly; *callant and loon* – young man; *scoup* –
ladle; *menzie* – household; *abeigh* – aloof; *elshin, lingle,
birse* – shoemaker's tools; *Forest* – Selkirkshire or Ettrick
Forest; *leal* – loyal; *Merse* – Berwickshire or Merse

There is a dispute about the origin of this ballad, some
suggesting that it is about a football match between the
families of Philiphaugh and Home (the family colours
of Home are green and yellow) but it is more likely that
it describes the Battle of Flodden and compares the
conduct of the Guildsmen of Selkirk with that of Lord
Home and his men. Some eighty souters or shoe-
makers of Selkirk fought bravely at Flodden in 1513,
their leader, the town clerk William Brydone being
knighted on the battlefield. Few survived. Lord Home
and his men routed the division of Sir Edmund
Howard, but could not reach the King, because of
English cavalry. Unable to advance, Lord Home left
the battle early and was subsequently blamed for the
King's death.

Each burgh in Scotland was famous for a particular
craft. Selkirk's was shoemaking. The granting of the

freedom of the burgh involves a curious ritual even today, whereby four or five bristles used in shoemaking are attached to the seal of the burgess ticket, dipped into wine, then passed between the lips as a token of respect for the Souters of Selkirk.

CHARLIE IS MY DARLING

'Twas on a Monday morning,
Right early in the year,
When Charlie came to our toun,
The young Chevalier.

Oh, Charlie is my darling,
My darling, my darling;
Oh, Charlie is my darling,
The young Chevalier.

As he came marching up the street,
The pipes play'd loud and clear,
And a' the folk came running out
To meet the Chevalier.

Oh, Charlie is my darling, &c.

Wi' Hieland bonnets on their heads,
And claymores bright and clear,
They came to fight for Scotland's right,
and the young Chevalier.

Oh, Charlie is my darling, &c.

They've left their bonnie Hieland hills,
Their wives and bairnies dear,
To draw the sword for Scotland's lord,
The young Chevalier.

Oh, Charlie is my darling, &c.

Oh, there were mony beating hearts,
And mony a hope and fear,
And mony were the prayers put up
For the young Chevalier.

Oh, Charlie is my darling, &c.

Chevalier – a favourite son

There are quite a few versions of this song, but that of Lady Nairne seems most appropriate, because of her family's Jacobite sympathies. Here she would have us imagine the sons of Scotland rushing from their homes in Highland regalia with swords drawn, to support Prince Charles Edward Stuart. Her family, the Oliphants of Gask were arch-Jacobite supporters. Lawrence Oliphant was Governor of Perth in 1745 when it was the Jacobite base, and his son Lawrence was an aide-de-camp to Charles on the march to Derby. The set of silver-gilt rococo cutlery used in that campaign by the Prince was a gift from the House of Gask. White roses, the Jacobite symbol, were grown in profusion at Gask and used to celebrate the royal birthdays.

THE BORDER WIDOW'S LAMENT

My love he built me a bonny bower,
And clad it a' wi' lilye flour;
A brawer bower ye ne'er did see,
Than my true love he built for me.

There came a man, by middle day,
He spied his sport, and went away;
And brought the King that very night,
Who brake my bower, and slew my knight.

He slew my knight, to me sae dear;
He slew my knight, and poin'd his gear;
My servants all for life did flee,
And left me in extremitie.

I sew'd his sheet, making my mane;
I watch'd the corpse, myself alane;
I watch'd his body night and day;
No living creature came that way.

I took his body on my back,
And whiles I gaed, and whiles I sat;
I digg'd a grave, and laid him in,
And happ'd him with the sod sae green.

But think na ye my heart was sair,
When I laid the moul' on his yellow hair;
O think na ye my heart was wae,
When I turn'd about, away to gae?

Nae living man I'll love again,
Since that my lovely knight is slain;
Wi' ae lock of his yellow hair
I'll chain my heart for evermair.

poin'd – made forfeit; *mane* – moan; *happ'd* – covered;
moul' – soil

This adaptation of the old English ballad 'The Lady Turned Serving - Man' tells of the execution in 1529 of Cockburn of Henderson, a noted Border freebooter. In an attempt to stamp out marauding bands in the region, Kings James V took part in rounding up the chief offenders. It is traditionally maintained that while having dinner Cockburn was surprised by the King and there and then hanged over the gate of his own tower. (The facts are that he was tried, convicted and beheaded in Edinburgh and his head displayed on the Tolbooth.) Swift action was also taken against many others, including Johnie Armstrong and Adam Scott of Tushielaw also known as King of the Border or King of Thieves.

After her husband's execution, Lady Cockburn attempted drowning herself in the Henderland Burn, a fast-flowing torrent running through the Dow-glen near the castle. The spot is marked and known as the 'Lady's Seat'. Traces of the castle can still be seen near the mouth of the River Megget in Selkirkshire. In the family burial ground, which once surrounded the chapel of the castle, stands a monument to Cockburn and his wife. The inscription reads:

HERE LYES PERYS OF COKBURNE
AND HIS WYFE MARJORY

Scott has cast doubt on this being their memorial, suggesting the stone is of a much older date and stating that the border raider's name was William.

THE QUEEN'S MARIE

Marie Hamilton's to the kirk gane,
Wi' ribbons on her hair;
The King thought mair o' Marie Hamilton,
Than ony that were there.

She hadna been about the King's court
A month, but barely one,
Till she was beloved by a' the King's court,
And the King the only man.

She hadna been about the King's court
A month, but barely three,
Till frae the King's court Marie Hamilton,
Marie Hamilton durstna be.

The King is to the Abbey gane,
To pu' the Abbey tree,
To scale the babe frae Marie's heart;
But the thing it wadna be.

O she has row'd it in her apron,
And set it on the sea, —
'Gae sink ye, or swim ye, bonny babe,
Ye'se get na mair o' me.'

Word is to the kitchen gane,
And word is to the ha',
And word is to the noble room,
Amang the ladyes a',
That Marie Hamilton's brought to bed,
And the bonny babe's mist and awa'.

'Get up, get up, Marie Hamilton:
Get up, and follow me;
For I am going to Edinburgh town,
A rich wedding for to see.'

The Queen was clad in scarlet,
Her merry maids all in green;
And every town that they cam to,
They took Marie for the Queen.

'Why weep ye so, ye burgess wives,
Why look ye so on me?
O, I am going to Edinburgh town,
A rich wedding for to see.'

When she gaed up the tolbooth stairs,
The corks frae her heels did flee;
And lang or e'er she cam down again,
She was condemn'd to die.

'Yestreen the Queen had four Maries,
The night she'll hae but three;
There was Marie Seaton, and Marie Beaton,
And Marie Carmichael, and me.

'O, often have I dress'd my Queen,
And put gold upon her hair;
But now I've gotten for my reward
The gallows to be my share.

'O little did my mother ken,
The day she cradled me,
The lands I was to travel in,
Or the death I was to die!'

Knox's *History of the Reformation* records that a
French woman of the Queen's chamber gave birth to
an illegitimate child. She and the father, the court
apothecary, murdered the baby and were
subsequently hanged in public, in Edinburgh. The
ballad is based upon this event.

The characters have somewhat changed with the

passage of time, Lord Darnley being substituted for the apothecary and Mary Hamilton for the lady of the bedchamber. The mention of the Queen's Maries is an attempt to locate the tale during the reign of Mary Queen of Scots, but although Mary was well aware of Darnley's infidelities at court, there is no evidence to support the substitution. Interestingly the same crime occurred at the court of Catherine of Russia. A Miss Hambleton, one of the Queen's favourites, was put to death for the murder of her three children in babyhood. For some time it was believed that this was the source of the ballad.

Many songs were written about the Queen's Maries and life at Queen Mary's court, and perhaps because of this different versions have become intermingled, some radically different from others. This selection of verses from the ballad gives the basis of the tale.

THE BONNIE HOUSE O' AIRLIE

It fell on a day, and a bonnie summer-day,
When green grew aits and barley,
That there fell out a great dispute,
Between Argyll and Airlie.

Argyll has raised an hunder men,
An hunder harness'd rarely;
And he's awa' by the back o' Dunkeld,
To plunder the castle o' Airlie.

Lady Ogilvie looks o'er her bower window,
And O, but she looks weary,
And there she spied the great Argyll,
Come to plunder the bonnie house o' Airlie.

'Come down, come down, my Lady Ogilvie,
Come down and kiss me fairly.'
'O, I wadna kiss the fause Argyll,
Though ye should na leave a standing stane in
Airlie.'

He has taken her by the left shoulder,
Says, 'Dame, where lies thy dowry?'
'O it's east and west yon wan water-side,
And it's down by the banks o' the Airlie.'

They hae sought it up, they hae sought it doun,
They hae sought it maist severely;
Till they fand it in the fair plum-tree,
That stands on the bowling-green o' Airlie.

He has taen her by the middle sae sma',
And O, but she grat sairly!
And he's set her down by the bonny burnside,
Till they plundered the castle of Airlie.

'O, I hae seven braw sons,' she says;
'The youngest ne'er saw his daddie;
But though I had an hundred mae,
I'd gie them a' to King Charlie!'

'But gin my gude lord had been at hame,
As this nicht he is wi' Charlie,
There durst na a Campbell in a'. the west,
Hae plunder'd the bonnie house o' Airlie!'

aits – oats; *grat* – wept

During the civil war in the 17th century, the Roman Catholic Earl of Airlie supported Charles I. Fear of being forced to sign the National Covenant made him flee Scotland, leaving the fortified stronghold of Airlie Castle in the capable hands of his son Lord Ogilvy. In 1640 the castle was besieged by the Earls of Montrose and Kinghorne, but when they failed to take it the Commission of Estates turned to the Earl of Argyle. An old enemy of Airlie, Argyll took up the task with relish. With 5,000 men he marched on the castle, first pillaging, then burning and finally razing it to the ground. One account by James Gordon, parson of Rothiemay tells of Argyll, 'taking a hammer in his hand, and knocking down the hewed work of the doors and windows, till he did sweat for heat at his work'.

Ogilvy escaped to Forther Castle where his pregnant wife was living, but Argyll followed, turned her out of doors, even refusing permission for her grandmother, Lady Drummie, to take her into her home at Kelly. Forther was also pillaged and razed, but not before the Campbells had occupied it for some months.

The scene of the ballad, because of the appearance of Lady Ogilvy, would seem to be Forther and not Airlie. There are many airs to fit the lyrics, the most commonly known, although probably not the best, being 'The Bonnie Banks o' Loch Lomond'. There could be confusion between 'The Bonnie House o' Airlie' and 'Young Airly'. Both mention 'Charlie', but whereas here we are talking about Charles I 'Young Airly' refers to 'Bonnie Prince Charlie' or Prince Charles Edward Stuart. A later Lord Ogilvy and his wife took an important part in the '45.

THE FLOWERS OF THE FOREST

I've heard them lilting, at the ewe milking,
Lasses a' lilting, before dawn of day;
But now they are moaning, on ilka green loaning;
The flowers of the forest are a' wede awae.

At bughts, in the morning, nae blithe lads
    are scorning;
Lasses are lonely, and dowie, and wae;
Nae daffing, nae gabbing, but sighing and sabbing;
Ilk ane lifts her leglin, and hies her awae.

In har'st, at the shearing, nae youths now are jeering;
Bandsters are runkled, and lyart or gray;
At fair, or at preaching, nae wooing, nae fleeching;
The flowers of the forest are a' wede awae.

At e'en, in the gloaming, nae younkers are roaming
'Bout stacks, with the lasses at bogle to play;
But ilk maid sits dreary, lamenting her deary —
The flowers of the forest are weded awae.

Dool and wae for the order, sent our lads to the
    Border!
The English, for ance, by guile wan the day;
The flowers of the forest, that fought aye the
    foremost,
The prime of our land, are cauld in the clay.

We'll hear nae mair lilting, at the ewe milking;
Women and bairns are heartless and wae:
Sighing and moaning, on ilka green loaning —
The flowers of the forest are a' wede awae.

green loaning – milking green; *wede awae* – vanished;
bughts – sheep pens; *dowie* – gloomy; *wae* – sad; *daffing* –
flirting; *gabbing* – chatting; *leglin* – milk pail; *har'st* – harvest;
bandster – sheaf-binder; *runkled* – wrinkled; *lyart* – streaked
with grey; *fleeching* – flattery; *younkers* – young men; *bogle*
– hide and seek; *dool* – sorrow

I've heard them lilt - in' at the ewe milk - in'
Lass - es a - lilt - in' be - fore dawn o' day. But now they are a moaning
il - ka green loan - in', The Flow'rs o' the For est are
a' wade a - wae

Jane Elliot, born in 1727, was the third daughter of Sir Gilbert Elliot, second baronet of Minto and Lord Justice-Clerk of Scotland. It is said that while driving home late one evening to Minto House, she and her brother Gilbert reflected on the damage done to the countryside and the people of Ettrick by the Battle of Flodden, where 10,000 Scots perished with their leader James IV. At Gilbert's suggestion Jane, there and then, began to compose new lyrics to fit this ancient air. She has created an elegiac tribute to the men of Ettrick Forest who fell at Flodden. It is a beautiful, haunting composition, lamenting the sadness and futility of war.

THE HUNDRED PIPERS

Wi' a hundred pipers an' a', an' a',
Wi' a hundred pipers an' a', an' a';
We'll up an' gie them a blaw, a blaw,
Wi' a hundred pipers an' a', an' a'.
Oh! it's owre the Border awa', awa',
It's owre the Border awa', awa',
We'll on and we'll march to Carlisle ha',
Wi' its yetts, its castell, an' a', an' a'.

Oh! our sodger lads looked braw, looked braw,
Wi' their tartans, kilts, an' a' an' a',
Wi' their bonnets, an' feathers, an' glittering gear,
An' pibrochs sounding sweet and clear.
Will they a' return to their ain dear glen?
Will they a' return, our Hieland men?
Second-sighted Sandy looked fu' wae,
And mothers grat when they marched away.

   Wi' a hundred pipers an' a', an' a',
   Wi' a hundred pipers an' a', an' a',
   We'll up and gie them a blaw, a blaw,
   Wi' a hundred pipers an' a, an' a'.

Oh wha is foremost o' a', o' a',
Oh wha does follow the blaw, the blaw?
Bonnie Charlie, the king o' us a', hurra!
Wi' his hundred pipers an' a, an' a'.
His bonnet an' feather, he's wavin' high,
His prancin steed maist seems to fly,
The nor' wind plays wi' his curly hair,
While the pipers blaw in an unco flare.

   Wi' a hundred pipers, & c.

The Esk was swollen, sae red and sae deep,
But shouther to shouther the brave lads keep;
Twa thousand swam owre to fell English ground,
An danced themselves dry to the pibroch's sound.
Dumfounder'd, the English saw-they-saw-
Dumfounder'd, they heard the blaw, the blaw;
Dumfounder'd, they a' ran awa', awa',
From the hundred pipers an' a', an' a.

   Wi' a hundred pipers, & c.

59

Prince Charles marched into Carlisle behind his 100 pipers on 18 November 1745, but his success was short-lived. The fortress of Carlisle was taken with remarkable ease, but in just over a month, on 20 December, his soldiers were swimming over the Esk in retreat, not advancing in splendour, as the song suggests. The Jacobites had managed to penetrate the English defences as far as Derby, before his generals advised Charles to turn back. He blamed lack of support from English Jacobites and a deafening silence from the French as the cause of his defeat, but in reality the French had never agreed to help and in Scotland itself he had as many opponents as supporters.

The disaster at Culloden, where Cumberland's 9,000 well-fed, properly trained soldiers slaughtered half that number of starving, ill-equipped Scots, was the death-knell of Jacobitism. Charles escaped back to France, while many of his loyal supporters were executed. Rebellion in Scotland was still feared by the government and the military defences at Fort Augustus and Fort William were strengthened and rebuilt. Charles died in 1788, but the refrain from 'Will Ye No Come Back Again' symbolises the sense of finality felt by many Scots. Lamenting the loss of their natural king they lamented the loss of their nation.

WILL YE NO COME BACK AGAIN?

Bonnie Charlie's now awa',
Safely owre the friendly main;
Mony a heart will break in twa,
Should he ne'er come back again.

   Will ye no come back again?
   Will ye no come back again?
   Better lo'ed ye canna be
   Will ye no come back again?

Ye trusted in your Hieland men,
They trusted you, dear Charlie;
They kent you hiding in the glen,
Your cleadin' was but barely.

    Will ye no, & c.

English bribes were a' in vain,
An' e'en tho' puirer we may be;
Siller canna buy the heart
That beats aye for thine and thee.

    Will ye no, & c.

We watched thee in the gloamin' hour,
We watched thee in the mornin' gray;
Tho' thirty thousand pounds they'd gi'e,
Oh there was nane that wad betray.

    Will ye no, & c.

Sweet's the laverock's note and lang,
Lilting wildly up the glen;
But aye to me he sings ae sang,
Will ye no come back again?

    Will ye no, & c.

cleadin – clothes; *laverock* – lark

CELEBRATION

RATTLIN', ROARIN' WILLIE

O rattlin', roarin' Willie,
O he held to the fair;
An' for to sell his fiddle,
And buy some other ware;
But parting wi' his fiddle,
The saut tear blin't his e'e;
And rattlin', roarin' Willie
Ye're welcome hame to me!

O Willie, come sell your fiddle,
O sell your fiddle sae fine;
O Willie, come sell your fiddle,
And buy a pint o' wine.
'If I should sell my fiddle,
The warld would think I was mad;
For mony a rantin' day
My fiddle and I hae had.'

As I cam by Crochallan,
I cannily keekit ben:
Rattlin', roarin' Willie
'Was sitting at yon boord'-en' —
Sitting at yon boord-en'
And amang gude companie;
Rattlin', roarin' Willie,
Ye're welcome hame to me!

saut – salt; *blin't* – blinded; *rantin'* – riotous; *keekit ben* –
peeped inside; *boord-en* – table-end

Robert Burns added the final verse to this old drinking
song as a tribute to his friend William Dunbar, an
Edinburgh solicitor. Dunbar was a fellow member and a
'colonel' in the 'Crochallan Fencibles', a club of wits
formed at a time when a 'home guard' was being raised
all over the country, although it would appear that the
chief purpose of this 'regiment' was raising glasses to
wage war on drink.

O THE EWE-BUGHTING'S BONNIE

O the ewe-bughting's bonnie, both e'ening and
   morn,
When our blithe shepherds play on the bogreed and
   horn;
While we're milking they're lilting sae jocund and
   clear;
But my heart's like to break when I think on my
   dear!

O the shepherds take pleasure to blow on the
   horn,
To raise up their flocks i' the fresh simmer morn;
On the steep ferny banks they feed pleasant and
   free –
But alas! my dear heart, all my sighing's for thee!

O the sheep-herding's lightsome amang the green
   braes,
Where Cayle wimples clear 'neath the white-
   blossomed slaes,
Where the wild-thyme and meadow-queen scent the
   saft gale,
And the cushat croods leesomely down in the dale.

There the lintwhite and mavis sing sweet frae the
   thorn,
And blithe lilts the laverock aboon the green corn,
And a' things rejoice in the simmer's glad prime —
But my heart's wi' my love in the far foreign clime.

ewe-bught – sheep pen; *bogreed* – reed-pipe; *wimples* –
meanders; *slaes* – sloes; *meadow-queen* – Spirea; *cushat*
– wood-pigeon; *croods* – coos; *lintwhite* – linnet; *mavis* –
song-thrush; *laverock* – lark

Thomas Pringle (1789-1834) wrote this song, which
originally consisted of two stanzas each with eight lines.
Here it has been divided into four verses. The first verse
he took from a fragment of a song written by Lady Grizell
Baillie, enclosed in a letter to her brother Patrick. At that

time Patrick and their father Sir Patrick Hume, later the Earl of Marchmont, were in exile in Holland along with Grizell's future husband, George Baillie of Jerviswood. There is a similarity in style with her composition 'O were na my heart light, I wad dee'. Pringle made his own contribution in the same pastoral vein.

Lady Grizell Baillie (1665-1746) deserves a special mention. The eldest of 18 children, she was a formidable character. At the age of twelve she carried messages from her father to his friend Robert Baillie in prison in Edinburgh. The families were staunch Covenanters and when Baillie was executed Sir Patrick went into hiding. For a month he lay in a vault in an old church, Grizell taking him food every night and talking till dawn. Later she concealed him in the family home until it was no longer safe and they fled to Holland, taking Robert Baillie's son George with them. When William III sailed to England to become king, Sir Patrick and George Baillie sailed with him, their estates were restored and in 1691 Grizell became George's wife and mistress of Mellerstain House in Berwickshire, not the mansion we know today, but its predecessor. In 1725 with her husband she overlooked the foundations of the new Adam mansion, which was begun by William and finished by Robert much later in the century.

THE DUSTY MILLER

Hey the dusty miller,
And his dusty coat,
He will win a shilling,
Ere he spend a groat.
Dusty was the coat,
Dusty was the colour,
Dusty was the kiss
I gat frae the miller.

Hey the dusty miller,
And his dusty sack,
Leeze me on the calling,
Fills the dusty peck;
Fills the dusty peck,
Brings the pennie siller;
I wad gie my coatie
For the dusty miller.

Hey the merry miller,
As the wheel rins roun,
And the clapper claps,
My heart gies a stoun.
Water grinds the corn,
Water wins the siller;
When the dam is dry,
I daute wi' the miller.

groat – smallest silver coin; *leeze me on* – great pleasure;
stoun – pang; *daute* – caress

Work songs, previously sung while the work was
done, eventually became celebratory and were performed at ceilidhs and gatherings. Many are laden
with sexual innuendo and crowned with bawdy chor-
uses, none more so than those referring to the miller,
who has been the butt of satiric jibe, hinting lewdness
and dishonesty, since Chaucer's time. 'The Dusty
Miller' is one of the more clever and subtle variations
on a well worn theme. Burns edited this popular ancient air for the *Scots Musical Museum*, altering the
second verse slightly. The third verse is a later addition,
but is in keeping with the tone of the original.

GREEN GROW THE RASHES

There's nought but care on ev'ry han,
In ev'ry hour that passes, O:
What signifies the life o' man,
An' 'twere na for the lasses, O?

    Green grow the rashes, O;
    Green grow the rashes, O;
    The sweetest hours that e'er I spend,
    Are spent amang the lasses, O!

The warly race may riches chase,
An' riches still may fly them, O;
An' tho' at last they catch them fast,
Their hearts can ne'er enjoy them, O.

    Green grow, & c.

But gie me a canny hour at e'en,
My arms about my Dearie, O;
An' warly cares, an' warly men,
May a' gae tapsalteerie, O!

    Green grow, & c.

For you sae douce, ye sneer at this,
Ye're nought but senseless asses, O:
The wisest Man the warl' saw,
He dearly lov'd the lasses, O.

    Green grow, & c.

Auld nature swears the lovely dears
Her noblest work she classes, O,
Her prentice han' she try'd on man,
An' then she made the lasses, O.

    Green grow, & c.

warly – worldly; *tapsalteerie* – topsy-turvy; *douce* – solid or sober

There's nought but care on ev'·ry han', In ev'·ry hour that pass·es, O; What

sig·ni·fies the life o' man, An' twere·na for the lass·es, O?

Green grows the rash·es, O. Green grows the rash·es, O; The

sweet·est hours that e'er I spend, Are spent a·mang the lass·es, O!

In 1784 in his *Commonplace Book*, Robert Burns describes this song as an observance on the 'various species of young men' and divided them into two categories 'the brave and the merry'. The former he believed are either 'goaded on by the love of money' or 'whose darling wish it is to make a figure in the world'. The latter are 'the jovial lads, who have too much fire and spirit to have any settled rule of action, but without much deliberation follow the strong impulses of nature.' It is not difficult to see where his own sympathies lay! One of his earliest songs, it typifies his joy, devilment and celebration at simply being alive. The privations of his earlier life, working a poor farm with his father and brother, made all life's experiences particularly intense.

Jean Glover, the Kilmarnock songstress was best known for her performance of 'Green Grow the Rashes', but Burns also recorded for Johnson's *Scots Musical Museum* the following song, 'O'er the Moor Amang the Heather', which she insisted was her own. 'I took the song down from her singing as she was strolling with a slight-of-hand blackguard through the country' is Burns' description of the occasion. He suggested she was a lady of dubious morality and in the habit of thieving, but a great beauty with an excellent voice.

Born in Kilmarnock in 1758, · the daughter of a weaver, Jean Glover was seduced at an early age by the stage. Before the advent of the theatre, performers regularly visited Kilmarnock, appearing at fairs and celebrations or at Croft Lodge, a well-known meeting place. Jean eventually eloped with a magician and they subsequently spent their lives touring Scotland and Ireland until her death in 1801 at Letterkenny. Her beauty and her voice are well documented and Burns, while casting doubts on her character, was not oblivious to her talents.

O'ER THE MOOR AMANG THE HEATHER

Comin' thro' the Craigs o' Kyle,
Amang the bonnie blooming heather,
There I met a bonnie lassie
Keeping a' her yowes thegether.

   O'er the moor amang the heather,
   O'er the moor amang the heather,
   There I met a bonnie lassie
   Keeping a' her yowes thegether.

Says I, my dear, where is thy hame,
In moor or dale, pray tell me whether?
She says, I tent thae fleecy flocks,
That feed amang the blooming heather.

   O'er the moor, & c.

We laid us down upon a bank,
Sae warm and sunny was the weather;
She left her flocks at large to rove,
Amang the bonnie blooming heather.

    O'er the moor, & c.

While thus we lay she sang a sang,
Till echo rang a mile and farther;
And aye the burden o' the sang
Was – o'er the moor amang the heather.

    O'er the moor, & c.

She charm'd my heart, an aye sin syne,
I coudna think on ony ither:
By sea and sky she shall be mine!
The bonnie lass amang the heather.

    O'er the moor, & c.

yowes – ewes, sheep; *tent* – care for, tend; *ay sin syne* –
always since then

THE CALD KAIL OF ABERDEEN

The cald kail of Aberdeen,
Is warming at Strabogie,
I fear 'twill tine the heat o'er seen,
And ne'er fill up the cogie.

The lasses about Bogingicht,
Ther leems they are baith clene and light,
And if they are but girded tight,
They'll dance the reell of Bogie.

Wae Aberdeen fat did ye mean,
Sae young a lass to woo man?
I'm seer to her it is nae mows,
Fat ere it be to you man.

But women now are nae sae blate,
But they ken auld folks out of date;
And better playthings can they get,
Than castocks in Strabogie.

cald – repellent; *kail* – colewort or cabbage; *tine* – kindle;
cogie – bucket; *leems* – limbs; *girded* – held; *wae* – shame
on you; *fat* – what; *I'm seer* – I'm responsible for her; *nae
mows* – no joke; *blate* – simple; *castock* – pith or stalk of a
cabbage

It is supposed that the 'hero' being castigated here is Sir
George Gordon of Haddo, who became Earl of
Aberdeen in 1682. Bog of Gight or Bogengight was the
ancient seat of the Seton-Gordon family, whilst the Bogie
is an Aberdeenshire river. There can be little doubt that
in this version the Earl is the subject of the jest. He died in
1720 at the age of 83, long after his wife's death.
Between times he gained a reputation for flirting with the
young girls of the county. If the lyrics are true his success,
though limited, provided much ammunition for the
satirical jibes of this drinking song.

The original author is unknown and there are many
other versions of this ballad including one by Lady
Nairne. All are much less pithy and many vary quite

radically from the first. The following recorded by Burns, illustrates the change from the original bawdy song filled with sexual innuendo, to the later versions, where the female is reduced to interfering interloper, and drink is now the only desire!

There's cauld kail in Aberdeen,
And castocks in Strathbogie;
When ilka lad maun hae his lass,
Then, fye! gie me my coggie.

My coggie, Sirs, my coggie, Sirs,
I canna want my coggie;
I wadna gie my three-gird caup,
For a' the queans on Bogie.

There's Johnie Smith has got a wife
That scrimps him o' his coggie,
If she were mine, upon my life,
I wad douk her in a bogie.

My coggie, Sirs, & c.

coggie – cog, drinking cup; *three-gird caup* – wooden drinking vessel girded with three hoops; *queans* – young girls; *douk* – to duck

WHEN THE KYE COMES HAME

Come, all ye jolly shepherds
That whistle through the glen,
I'll tell ye of a secret
That courtiers dinna ken:
What is the greatest bliss
That the tongue o' man can name?
'Tis to woo a bonnie lassie
When the kye comes hame.

When the kye comes hame,
When the kye comes hame,
'Tween the gloaming and the mirk,
When the kye comes hame.

'Tis not beneath the coronet,
Nor canopy of state,
'Tis not on couch of velvet,
Nor arbour of the great —
'Tis beneath the spreading birk,
In the glen without the name,
Wi' a bonnie, bonnie lassie,
When the kye comes hame.

When the kye, & c.

When the blewart bears a pearl,
And the daisy turns a pea,
And the bonnie lucken gowan
Has fauldit up her e'e,
Then the laverock frae the blue lift
Drops down, an' thinks nae shame
To woo his bonnie lassie
When the kye comes hame.

When the kye, & c.

Then since all nature joins
In this love without alloy,
Oh, wha wad prove a traitor
To nature's dearest joy?
Or wha wad choose a crown,
Wi' its perils and its fame,
And miss his bonnie lassie
When the kye comes hame?

When the kye, & c.

kye – cows; *mirk* – dark; *birk* – birch; *blewart* – blue wort, small blue flower; *gowan* – daisy; *fauldit* – folded; *laverock* – lark; *lift* – sky

These are just a few verses from a song, which Hogg himself thought the song was too long to sing from beginning to end. Before he took hold of it and fastened it to a definitive time of day, the saying, 'When the Kye Comes Home' meant 'never'. Hogg turned it into a literal expression describing the short period between dusk and dark, when the cows wander home to the byre. In the country he was often assured that his interpretation was 'nonsense'.

Hogg had no recollection of having written it, until coming across a plagiarised and mangled version of it in someone else's writing. He there and then resolved to rewrite and improve the original. It became his favourite pastoral for singing and the tune is 'Shame fa' the gear and the blathrie o't'.

MY AIN FIRESIDE

O I ha'e seen great anes, and sat in great ha's,
'Mong lords and 'mong ladies a' cover'd wi' braws;
At feasts made for princes, wi' princes I've been,
Whare the grand shine o' splendour has dazzled
    my een;
But a sight sae delightfu' I trow, I ne'er spied,
As the bonnie blythe blink o' my ain fireside.
My ain fireside, my ain fireside,
O cheery's the blink o' mine ain fireside.

    My ain fireside, my ain fireside,
    O sweet is the blink o' my ain fireside.

Ance mair, gude be prais'd round my ain
    heartsome ingle,
Wi' the friends o' my youth I cordially mingle;
Nae forms to compel me to seem wae or glad,
I may laugh when I'm merry, and sigh when I'm
    sad.
Nae falsehood to dread, and nae malice to fear,
But truth to delight me, and friendship to cheer;
Of a' roads to happiness ever were tried,
There's nane half so sure as ane's ain fireside.

    My ain fireside, my ain fireside,
    O there's nought to compare wi' ane's ain fireside.

When I draw in my stool on my cosy hearthstane,
My hearts loups sae light I scarce ken't for my ain;
Care's down on the wind, it is clean out o' sight,
Past troubles they seem but as dreams of the night.
I hear but kend voices, kend faces I see,
And mark saft affection glent fond frae ilk e'e;
Nae fleetchings o' flattery, nae boastings of pride,
'Tis heart speaks to heart at ane's ain fireside.

    My ain fireside, my ain fireside,
    O there's nought to compare wi' ane's ain

braws – fine clothes; *trow* – to feel sure; *loups* – leaps;
glent – shine; *fleetchings* – flattery, fawning

Mrs Elizabeth Hamilton, the writer of this song, also produced various educational works and a successful novel, *The Cottagers of Glenburnie*. She was born in Belfast in 1758 of mixed Scottish and Irish descent, although her childhood was spent with an aunt near Stirling. Her brother Captain Charles Hamilton of the East India Company was also an author. She must have married early in life, but she lived most of her adult life single. A literary lady, with a wide circle of friends, she spent many years in Bath with her sister, before returning to Scotland in 1803 to live in Edinburgh. Many airs have been used with these lyrics, the oldest being 'Todlen Hame', which would certainly be in tune with the sentiments expressed in the lyrics.

MACPHERSON'S FAREWELL

Farewell, ye dungeons dark and strong,
The wretch's destinie!
MacPherson's time will not be long,
On yonder gallows-tree.

Sae rantingly, sae wantonly,
Sae dauntingly gae'd he:
He play'd a spring, and danc'd it round,
Below the gallows-tree.

O what is death but parting breath?
On mony a bloody plain
I've dar'd his face, and in this place
I scorn him yet again!

Sae rantingly & c.

Untie these bands from off my hands,
And bring to me my sword;
And there's no a man in all Scotland,
But I'll brave him at a word.

Sae rantingly & c.

I've liv'd a life of sturt and strife;
I die by treacherie:
It burns my heart I must depart,
And not avengèd be. ·

Sae rantingly & c.

Now farewell light, thou sunshine bright,
And all beneath the sky!
May coward shame distain his name,
The wretch that dares not die!

Sae rantingly, & c.

sturt – trouble

This version of 'MacPherson's Farewell' or 'Rant' was composed by Burns in 1787. The original was written by James MacPherson as he waited to be executed at Banff in 1700. A well-known Highland freebooter, he was also an excellent musician. Just before he was hanged, standing below the gallows tree, he sang and played the tune on his violin. He then offered the instrument to anyone in the crowd, who would play the song at his wake. His last wish refused, his final furious dramatic gesture before flinging himself from the ladder to his death, was to dash the violin to pieces on the executioner's head. MacPherson's own version of the song can still be seen in old collections, but Burns seems to have encapsulated the bravado of the man, his disdain for life and his contempt for society.

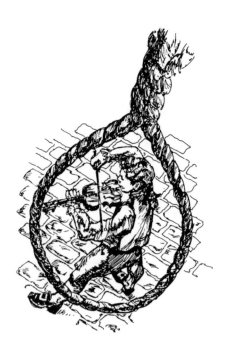

COMIN' THRO' THE RYE

Comin' thro' the rye, poor body,
Comin' thro' the rye;
She draigl't a' her petticoatie,
Comin' thro' the rye.

Oh, Jenny's a' weet, poor body,
Jenny's seldom dry;
She draigl't a' her petticoatie,
Comin' thro' the rye.

Gin a body meet a body
Comin' thro' the rye;
Gin a body kiss a body
Need a body cry?

Oh, Jenny's a' weet, & c.

Gin a body meet a body
Comin' thro' the glen;
Gin a body kiss a body,
Need the warld ken?

Oh, Jenny's a' weet, & c.

draigl't – dirtied; *gin* – if

This is an old air improved and made popular by Burns. The 'rye' which Jenny is 'comin' thro'' has been the subject of much debate. Could it be the Rye Water near Dalry, which soaked Jenny's clothes as she waded through or was the Rye a muddy, wet lane leading down into the same town? The most likely explanation is that Burns was merely describing the sight of a young woman making her way through a field of rye. Then it becomes an evocative pastoral image of peace and plenty, the way many artists have chosen to depict the scene on canvas.

The modern version is altered and Jenny has become the singer of the song.

Ilka lassie has her laddie,
Nane they say ha'e I;
Yet a' the lads they smile at me
When comin' thro' the rye.

Chorus

FOR A' THAT AND A' THAT

Is there, for honest poverty
That hangs his head, and a' that?
The coward-slave, we pass him by —
We dare be poor for a' that!
For a' that, and a' that,
Our toils obscure, and a' that,
The rank is but the guinea's stamp —
The man's the gowd for a' that.

What though on hamely fare we dine —
Wear hoddin grey, and a' that?
Gie fools their silks, and knaves their wine —
A man's a man, for a' that;
For a' that, and a' that
Their tinsel show, and a' that;
The honest man, though e'er sae poor,
Is king o' men for a' that.

Ye see yon birkie ca'd a lord,
Wha struts, and stares, and a' that;
Though hundreds worship at his word,
He's but a coof for a' that:
For a' that, and a' that,
His ribband, star, and a' that;
The man of independent mind,
He looks and laughs at a' that.

A prince can mak' a belted knight,
A marquis, duke and a' that;
But an honest man's aboon his might,
Gude faith he mauna fa' that!
For a' that, and a' that,
Their dignities and a' that;
The pith o' sense, and pride o' worth,
Are higher rank than a' that.

Then let us pray that come it may,
As come it will for a' that,
That sense and worth, o'er a' the earth,
May bear the gree and a' that:
For a' that, and a' that,
It's coming' yet for a' that,
That man to man, the warld o'er,
Shall brothers be for a' that!

gowd – gold; *hoddin* – coarse cloth; *birkie* – lively youth;
coof – a fool; *mauna fa' that* – must not try that; *gree* –
prize

Is there for hon-est po-ver-ty, That hangs his head and a' that? The
cow-ard slave we pass him by; We dare be poor, for a' that! For
a'____ that and a'____ that, Our toils ob-scure and a' that; The
rank is but the guin-ea stamp, The man's the gowd for a' that.

Robert Burns was not a revolutionary in the true sense of
the word, but he might have been seen as such by the
society he ridicules in this satirical song, written in 1795
shortly before he died. By then he had been taken up
and dropped by Edinburgh's *beau monde*, his farm at
Ellisland had been abandoned, his final sad and sickly
days spent as a Customs and Excise Officer in Dumfries.
Behind the mocking tone and jaunty tune lies a sad
weariness with the world.

Robert Chambers, obviously with thoughts in mind of
the recent revolution in France, described the song as
'embodying all the false philosophy of Burns' time and of
his own mind'. In contrast, Thomas Carlyle, looking
back on Burns' later years, sums up his worth thus:

There is reason to believe that, in his latter years,
the Dumfries aristocracy had partly withdrawn
themselves from Burns, as from a tainted person,
no longer worthy of their acquaintance. That
painful class, stationed in all provincial cities,
behind the outmost breast-work of gentility, there
to stand siege, and do battle against the intrusions
of grocerdom and grazierdom, had actually seen
dishonour in the society of Burns, and branded

84

him with their veto, – had, as we vulgarly say, cut him! Alas! when we think that Burns now sleeps 'where bitter indignation can no longer lacerate his heart', and that those fair dames and frizzled gentlemen already lie at his side, – where the breast-work of gentility is quite thrown down, – who would not sigh over the thin delusions and foolish toys that divide heart from heart, and make man unmerciful to his brother!

Thomas Carlyle,
1828.

KIRKDAMDIE FAIR

(A fragment)

O Robin lad, where hae ye been,
Ye look sae trig and braw, man;
Wi' ruffled sark, and neat and clean,
And Sunday coat and a', man.

Quo' Rab, I had a day to spare,
And I went to Kirkdamdie Fair,
Like mony anither gouk to stare,
At a' that could be seen, man.

The tents, in a' three score and three,
Were planted up and down, man,
While pipes and fiddles thro' the fair,
Gaed bummin' roun' and roun' man.

Here Jamie Brown and Mary Bell,
Were seated on a plank man,
Wi' Robin Small and Kate Dalziel,
And heartily they drank, man.

A country chap had got a drap,
And he guid thro' the fair, man;
He swore to face wi' twa three chiels,
He wadna muckle care, man.

At length he lent a chiel a clout,
Till his companions turned out,
So on they fell, wi' sic pell-mell,
Till some lay on the ground, man.

Some did the thieving trade pursue,
While ithers cam' to sell their woo';
And ithers cam' to weet their mou,
And gang wi' lasses hame, man.

trig – smart; *sark* – shirt; *gouk* – fool; *chiel* – a youth; *clout* –
blow

Kirkdamdie Fair was an annual event in Ayrshire and more like a medieval rural celebration than merely the buying and selling of goods. The author of the ballad is unknown, but he or she has left us with a vivid Hardy-esque image of country life as it was enjoyed on the last Saturday of May every year at Kirkdamdie. It was the only market serving a large district, and brought people from far and wide, including merchants and pedlars with wares from England and Europe. There was a large trade in wool and lambs, which latterly brought buyers from the English manufacturing towns, and some 30 or 40 stalls sold everything from clothing to ironmongery and provided amusements and refreshments for the crowds.

Traditionally at the end of the day new and old feuds were settled. This could end in a pitched battle of between one and two hundred men fighting with fists or sticks. In later years large numbers of Irishmen settled in Scotland at Girvan and around the coast, coming to Kirkdamdie purely for the pleasure of a fight, either amongst themselves or with the locals. Kirkdamdie Fair was known as the Donnybrook of Scotland, associating it with the fair held at Donnybrook in Ireland. Even today 'a donnybrook' is a vernacular term for a fight resembling a battle.

Smuggling was rife in Scotland after the Union in 1707, particularly in Ayrshire and Galloway. Hidden away in the south-west many of the local lairds organised and profited from this trade, without fear of the law. The fair was often used as a meeting place to distribute the spoils and plan future schemes.

The annual gathering today is separated from the trading aspects of the fair, which now take place at weekly auctions. Once a year, at County Shows held all over the countryside, prizes are awarded for the best stock. The stalls still provide amusement and refreshment, the only battles now being canine ones at the dog show. Like the seasons, it is still a rural ritual that celebrates the year past and looks forward to the future.

AULD LANG SYNE

Should auld acquaintance be forgot
And never brought to mind?
Should auld acquaintance be forgot,
And auld lang syne?

   For auld lang syne, my dear,
   For auld lang syne,
   We'll tak' a cup o' kindness yet,
   For auld lang syne.

And surely ye'll be your pint-stoup,
And surely I'll be mine;
And we'll tak' a cup o' kindness yet,
For auld lang syne.

   For auld & c.

We twa hae run about the braes,
And pou'd the gowans fine;
But we've wander'd mony a weary fit,
Sin' auld lang syne.

   For auld & c.

We twa hae paidl'd in the burn,
Frae morning sun till dine;
But seas between us braid hae roar'd,
Sin' auld lang syne.

   For auld & c.

And there's a hand, my trusty fiere!
And gie's a hand o' thine!
And we'll tak' a right gude-willie waught,
For auld lang syne.

   For auld & c.

lang syne – long since (ago); *pint-stoup* – pint measure; *fit* – foot; *braid* – broad; *fiere* – friend; *gude-willie waught* – hearty large drink

'Auld Lang Syne' sums up the essence of balladry and song. Meaning the days of long ago or old friendship, it celebrates the simpler, more spontaneous moments in life. The symbolic joining of hands at the end, links not only those present, but the present to the past; for that moment the lost magic of the old ballads flickers. The third and fourth verses are by Burns, the others very old. He said of it: 'this old song and tune has often thrilled through my soul.'

Bibliography

Aytoun, William, *The Ballads of Scotland*, Vols 1-II, William Blackwood & Sons, 1858

Bold, Alan, *The Ballad*, Methuen, 1979

Burnett, George, *A Book of Border Verse*, Blackie, 1926

Chambers, Robert, *The Scottish Ballads*, William Tait, 1829

Crawford, Thomas, *Society and the Lyric*, Scottish Academic Press, 1979

Cromek, R.H., *Remains of Nithsdale and Galloway Song*, T. Cadell & W. Davies, 1810

Cunningham, Allan, *The Songs of Scotland*, Vols I-IV, John Taylor, 1825

Douglas, William Scott (ed.), *The Poetical Works of Robert Burns* (Kilmarnock Edition), John Menzies, D. Brown, 1923

Graham, George F., *The Songs of Scotland*, Vols I-III, Wood, 1848

Hogg, James, *The Jacobite Relics of Scotland*, Vols I-II, William Blackwood, T. Cadell & W. Davis, 1819

Lenman, Bruce, *The Jacobite Cause*, Richard Drew, 1986

Paterson, James (ed.) *The Ballads and Songs of Ayrshire*, John Dick, 1846

Rogers, Charles (ed.) *The Life and Songs of the Baroness Nairne*, John Grant, 1896

Scott, Sir Walter, *Minstrelsy of the Scottish Border*, Vols I-IV, Oliver & Boyd, 1932